BEING KNOWN AND
BEING REVEALED

The Julian Hartt Library
Series Editor
Jonathan R. Wilson

****

Toward a Theology of Evangelism
Being Known and Being Revealed
The Lost Image of Man
Theology and the Church in the University
A Christian Critique of American Culture
The Restless Quest
Theological Method and Imagination
What We Make of the World: Memoirs of Julian Hartt

BEING KNOWN AND BEING REVEALED

BY

JULIAN N. HARTT

Wipf & Stock
PUBLISHERS
Eugene, Oregon

Wipf and Stock Publishers
199 W 8th Ave, Suite 3
Eugene, OR 97401

Being Known and Being Revealed
By Hartt, Julian N.
Copyright©1957 by Hartt, Julian N.
ISBN: 1-59752-913-3
Publication date 9/11/2006
Previously published by Pacific Philosophy Institute, 1957

Series Foreword

Why is Wipf and Stock reprinting the works of Julian Hartt? Certainly his faculty appointments and administrative responsibilities at Yale (1943-1972) and Virginia (1972-1981), after an initial term at Berea, indicate something of his participation in a formative period for American theological education. That observation, however, does not identify the impact of his work or the reasons for reprinting his books. His work deserves reprinting and renewed attention for at least four reasons.

One reason for reprinting Hartt's work is the depth of theological reflection represented in it. The books are not easy to enter. They are densely packed and cannot be read quickly. My first encounter with his work occurred in the basement of the library at the University of British Columbia. I was browsing in the religion section and was drawn to a book by its aesthetic appeal. Its size and proportions as well as its dusty blue color drew me in. I could not read the title on its spine, so I took it off the shelf: *A Christian Critique of American Culture*. Intrigued, I borrowed it from the library and renewed the loan several times while I managed to read about one-third of the book. I finally returned the book to the library and did not read it again until many years later.

So, let's be clear. Hartt's work makes significant demands on readers. His own erudition and his ability to bring it together in concentrated form means that his work cannot be skimmed for the "high points." Every book is packed with high points. Each paragraph makes an important contribution to the argument or exposition. Hartt's books, then, are not quick and easy reads. But such characteristics also mean that reading carefully through one of Hartt's books teaches more than sprinting through numerous other works. In an age that values short paragraphs, shallow thinking, and predigested ideas (that is, pablum), Hartt's books are strong meat not thin gruel.

Our age needs the kind of work that makes us slow down, chew on a sentence, a paragraph, an argument, until it has nourished our lives. That's what Hartt's work provides for us.

A second reason for making Hartt's work more readily available is not just its character but also its content. Hartt's work is not only densely packed, it is also sharply penetrating. One of Hartt's friends told me about once hearing him preach in a British Methodist church on Good Friday. "I felt like I had been laid bare, stripped of every pretense, lacerated by the truth, so that I could be healed by the gospel."

In Hartt's work, readers will find a severe truth-telling grounded in the conviction that only the truth revealed in Christ will set us free. So Hartt's penetrating insight and prophetic truth strips away our platitudes and the thin lies that we wrap around ourselves to protect us from the admission that our emptiness and anxiety go to our very core. Even though—perhaps precisely because—Hartt exposes these lies in their particular cultural expressions, his severity continues to administer healing grace to us today. Our particular cultural expressions of the lies and illusions that we create for ourselves may differ, but our propensity to live by lies and illusions remains a part of every human condition.

We must go one step further to understand why the content of Hartt's work is so penetrating. Its power lies not only in his clear-eyed perception of the lies we live by; even more, the power of his work lies in his apprehension of the gospel of Jesus Christ. My use of the word *apprehension* here is very important. Hartt has been apprehended by the gospel, and in the outworking of that gospel in his life, he has also apprehended it. This notion of apprehension is crucial to Hartt's thinking. Though he had this understanding of apprehension early in his intellectual development, it is highly developed in the work of Austin Farrer, who contributed significantly to Hartt's thinking. Today, a similar notion may be found in Reinhard Hütter's notion (in *Suffering Divine Things*) of being "rapt" by God.

For Hartt, to be apprehended by the gospel is to be so captured by God's grace in Jesus Christ that all things are seen by its light. All of our "unreality systems" are exposed as antihuman distortions of the way to human flourishing. So the gospel of Jesus Christ discloses the Rule of God in which we truly find the flourishing of all creation. Without this conviction, Hartt's brilliant exposure of our lies plunges us into despair. But in the light of the good news that Jesus Christ has overcome all that we fear, all that we deny, all our anxieties, all Sin, we are now free to confess the truth of our sin because the grace of God is greater still.

This double-edged truth makes Hartt's theology an invaluable witness to our age. We seem to combine cynicism about intentions in the exercise of human powers with a fatalism about the inevitability of misguided optimism that "this one time" we will achieve our intentions, which, when achieved, turn out not to be our salvation but our continuing damnation—and that by our own hands. In the midst of such darkness and despairing, the light and hope of Christ announce God's salvation for a damned humanity.

Hartt's perceptive and profound witness to this good news illuminates our world, penetrates the armor of lies, breaks the chains of sin, and sets us free to follow Christ. For these reasons, his work equips us for the mission to which the Lord and Savior of the church has called us.

A third reason for reprinting and reading Hartt's work is his impact on North American theology. Although Hartt is not well-known, during his twenty-nine years at Yale and ten years at Virginia he exercised enormous influence on a whole generation of theologians. Hartt himself had relatively few doctoral students. Many suggest that his high standards and fierce rhetoric put many students off. Hartt was a skilled debater who appears to have seldom adjusted his style according to circumstance. During Hartt's years at Yale, the school produced a majority of North America's theologians for a generation. Many of these theologians have acknowledged to me in private correspondence that Hartt's influence upon them is strong even if they do not consider themselves to be one of Hartt's students. (There is also the untold and controversial role that Hartt played in a struggle over control of the graduate program in religion.)

But there are also many who trained or taught at Yale and Virginia who have publicly acknowledged Hartt's impact: Diogenes Allen, Stephen Crites, James Gustafson, David Bailey Harned, Ray Hart, Van Harvey, Stanley Hauerwas, Gordon Kaufman, Walter Lowe, and John Sykes. Anyone who knows the work of these men (and most of the graduates in those days were men; one notable exception is Sallie McFague who was a student of H. Richard Niebuhr but who also served as teaching assistant to Hartt) will be intrigued by Hartt's role in their work. Two of Hartt's greatest fans are James Gustafson and Stanley Hauerwas, whose theologies have developed along quite divergent paths. For Hartt to be acknowledged by such influential and wildly diverse thinkers means that his work deserves careful attention.

Moreover, Hartt's work has received attention from contemporary Anabaptist and Baptist theologians. John Howard Yoder references Hartt's work briefly and appreciatively. James Wm. McLendon, Jr., gives Hartt sustained attention in developing the last volume of his "baptist" theology, *Systematic Theology, Volume 3: Witness*.

Does this diversity mean that Hartt is hopelessly incoherent or so obscure that he can be taken to mean anything? Not at all. Rather, this diversity means that Hartt's thought is rich in depth and generous in its embrace. Hartt seemed to many of his peers to have read and assimilated everything, or almost everything, of importance to the work of theology. At the same time, he did not lose his creative powers. Thus, through the assimilative and creative power of his intellect he produces seminal work that contains the seeds of many fruitful theological endeavors.

Finally, we need Hartt's work available to us today because he wrote as a theologian for "America." Hartt grew up on the American prairies with Hubert Humphrey as his childhood friend. Like many he returned often to those wide-open skies that represented for him the possibilities of American culture. But given his clear-eyed perception of our lies and illusions and his apprehension of the truth of Jesus Christ, he also saw the cultural embodiment of anxiety that distorts and corrupts the flourishing of life in the human creation that we call America. Today, in the midst of the rise of "the American Empire," Hartt's prophetic and subtle analyses are more desperately needed than ever.

So, for these four reasons, at least, we need Hartt's witness to the gospel of Jesus Christ in our midst. In the seven volumes that make up "The Julian Hartt Library," a new generation of readers will have available to them the major works of this seminal "American" theologian. I have written the Introduction to this present volume. I wrote above about my first encounter with Hartt's work. I had set it aside by the time I arrived at Duke for graduate studies in 1986. In the course of preparing to write a dissertation on Austin Farrer under the guidance of Tom Langford, I discovered that Hartt had used Farrer's work in his classes at Yale. One evening, prior to the start of Stanley Hauerwas's Theological Ethics Seminar, I asked him if he thought that Hartt would be open to a visit from me to talk about Farrer's work. "Sure," he said. "But you know you should think about writing on Julian. No one has taken a close look at him." With Tom Langford's encouragement, that's what I did. Writing on Hartt and continuing to draw on his work for my own vocation has been a wonderful adventure. I am grateful to Julian Hartt for the work he has done, to Stanley Hauerwas for his insight, to Tom Langford for his guidance, and to Wipf and Stock for their impetus to republish these works.

Jonathan R. Wilson
Acadia Divinity College, 2005

INTRODUCTION

Now I a fourfold vision see,
And a fourfold vision is given to me;
'Tis fourfold in my supreme delight
And threefold in soft Beulah's night
And twofold Always. May God us keep
From Single vision & Newton's sleep! [1]

This is a bold book. It aims to retrieve a richer, more generous understanding of the world than is common in much of modern thought. It seeks to save us from the narrow-

---

[1] Hartt's determination to keep first things first is reflected in his repeated italicizing of the "*moment*," with respect to which specific, articulated truths are secondary "derivatives" (54). There is nothing inherently wrong with the latter, but God retains God's freedom with respect to them (54md). This freedom is reflected in the fact that as surely as being reveals itself, so too it "re-veils" itself (54bt). Note that in this veiling, being retains an agency. It remains active, only in another mode, viz. the act of veiling itself. Thus when mystery recedes (55tp), it is not simply the result of institutionalization, as if the power of being had been canceled and social conventions had complete control. Rather it may be said (in my words, not Hartt's) that being itself retains its own freedom (cf. transcendence), which now shows itself in another mode—as the human cry in the face of despair and meaninglessness (55md). But this also means that we can say, more positively, that in "being self-disclosed in revelation" God is not restricted or compromised. Revelation does not lessen divine mystery and freedom. Entirely to the contrary, God is in God's own being "the perfection of freedom" (55bt). William Blake, *The Letters of William Blake,* ed. Geoffrey Keynes (Cambridge: Harvard University Press, 1970), 62. "Beulah's night" refers to a place of rest and replenishment.

ness of what the poet William Blake calls "Single vision & Newton's sleep." In short, it offers an intellectual liberation. For, in Julian Hartt's words, we need to be freed "from certain ghosts that haunt the distinction between subjective and objective being; and from that particular ghost . . . which chatters about the superior reality of the objective over the subjective" (9).

We live in a world that suffers from what many have called "the subject-object split." This is the supposed gap between the realm of scientific facts "outside" ourselves and the realm of personal feelings "inside" ourselves. Feeling a sense of disconnection, many people hunger for a more healing, holistic vision of the world—for something like Blake's "fourfold vision." In the present book, Julian Hartt sets out to recover just such a vision. And if there is one secret to the way he does this, it lies in the word "*being*." To write an entire book about being goes against our normal expectations. We tend to think of "being" (if we think of it at all) as the most general, abstract, and therefore the most empty of terms. In these pages Hartt awakens us to the possibility that "being" may be—potentially—the deepest and richest of terms. Otherwise put, the concept of being may be uniquely qualified to provide us as *a way into* the depth and richness that is so wanting in our modern, ghost-ridden existence.

The trick is not to think of "being" in abstraction. The trick is to appreciate that the term is in fact profoundly *relational*. "Being," by its very nature, overcomes our sense of disconnectedness. This is why Hartt makes "being" his key term, dealing first with being in relation to knowing

Chap 1 ?

and in relation to revealing (in chapters I–II and III–IV respectively). And where does all this lead? A high point in Hartt's vision of healing wholeness comes at the end of Chapter II, where he writes, "The appetite of the mind we call 'knowing' is an appetite satisfied only by being itself; and what holds for mind, holds for all our essentially human appetites" (33). Our minds are not just machines; they have living appetites. And the world is not indifferent to our hopes. Being itself, which seems so empty, is what ultimately speaks to the appetite—the desire, the need, the longing—of our minds. And as with the mind, so with "all our . . . human appetites"! In this sense, the living richness of being is, in Blake's words, our "supreme delight."[2]

To understand how this is so will, not surprisingly, require some effort of attention. To help ease the way, the remainder of the present Introduction will be devoted to a running commentary and paraphrase of Hartt's text. The difficulties which arise are, I think, no greater than the topic requires; and insofar as the difficulties derive from the topic, they themselves help us to understand it. As one

---

[2] A lovely, accessible introduction to this valuation of being is Josef Pieper, *The Silence of St. Thomas* (London: Faber and Faber, 1957) 62–75. Somewhat more technical but also illuminating and concise is David B. Burrell, *Knowing the Unknowable God: Ibn-Sina, Maimonides, Aquinas* (Notre Dame: University of Notre Dame Press, 1986) 29–34. The work of Étienne Gilson is of pivotal importance; for guidance, see Helen James John, "The Emergence of the Act of Existing in Recent Thomism," *International Philosophical Quarterly* II:4 (December 1962), 595–620. Also instructive for the general reader is Robert Sokolowski, *The God of Faith and Reason* (Notre Dame: University of Notre Dame Press, 1982) on "the Christian difference."

comes to see this, the book begins to open up. Regarding the extraordinary illumination the book affords, I will go ahead and make my grand claim. *Being Known and Being Revealed* performs a kind of intellectual therapy. In some fifty brief pages it puts us back in touch with the great tradition of Western thought that forms a sort of continuity from Plato through Aristotle, Athanasius, Aquinas and Dante. Moreover, it does this without pulling in an array of names and technical terms that might intimidate the average reader. Instead Hartt allows the tradition to unfold by its own internal logic, within the reader's mind. The relationships unfold and we find ourselves within them. We find ourselves restored to the richness and the depth of our heritage.

While some readers will begin with this introduction, others may wish to proceed directly to the text, referring back to the commentary as needed. Page references appear parenthetically in the text; to assist in locating specific passages, page numbers are sometimes accompanied by "tp," "md" and "bt" to indicate top, middle or bottom of the page. I need hardly add that my reading is but one possible interpretation of the text.

I. Being as the Object of Knowledge. The first two chapters deal with the two sides of the modern subject-object split. The chapter titles already indicate Hartt's way of overcoming the supposed split, for they speak of "Being as . . . Object . . ." and "Being as . . . Subject . . ." Being is primary; the subject-object distinction is real, springing from being, but it is not ultimate.

The first two paragraphs of Chapter I introduce not just the chapter but the entire book. Hartt alludes to the supposed split between the "external world" and the human mind, and then proceeds directly to those we may call the philosophers of "Single vision." These are those who believe they can know God by using the same "net" that they use to gain knowledge of common objects (7). They fail to recognize is that God may be different or "other" than such objects; and that the world itself may be richer and deeper than is dreamt of in their philosophies (cf. "Newton's sleep.") At the same time Hartt adds (8) that the otherness of God does not mean that there can be no relation between revelation and our (ordinary) ways of knowing. In fact, a common ground between being known and being revealed appears once we appreciate the "'back-world'" of implicit and often perfectly legitimate presuppositions that stands behind everyday religious discourse. Religious believers may not use the word "being," but they have to do with being, nevertheless.

On reflection (9) the very thing that makes us uneasy with the notion of being can be a virtue. This is an instance of how the difficulty—namely, the great abstractness of the term—fits the topic. For it is precisely its ability to be so abstract that makes "being" so comprehensive, and thus less partial or biased. Now the first thing to be said about being (10) is, as noted earlier, that it is relational. It connects, it overcomes splits. Seen through the prism of being, the world is not just a jar of marbles and human experience is not just (in a phrase that is not Hartt's) "one damn thing after another." Moreover, the comprehensiveness of "being" exceeds any narrow, partisan point of view. It is positively liberating, it sets the mind free (11). Specifically, we are freed of the disabling "doctrine of the greater reality of objective being" (11md), the damaging "ghost" noted at the beginning of this Introduction.

The task of intellectual ghost busting involves getting clear on what the term "objective being" does and does not imply. For something to be objectively does entail a certain independence, givenness or "thereness" (12tp). This "power" (12md) of thereness explains why objective being may seem more real than subjective being.[3] But a certain relative independence need not imply separation, as in the supposed subject-object split. For the tradition from which Hartt speaks, the ability to be (objectively) is ipso facto a power *to "communicate"* (12md). Moreover, the fact that the communicative power springs from the being's very be-ing means that the communication is deep. It is not just a "sense impression." In it the object makes accessible something of its inmost reality (13md).

Each being exercises a certain autonomy, "a kind of life to itself" and thereby a certain positive mystery (14.) In Gerard Manley Hopkins's phrase, "There lives the dearest freshness deep down things."[4] But because its power is

---

[3] It is helpful to distinguish objective being, i.e. the objective way or mode of being, from any particular (objective or subjective) being. Making the distinction reminds us that a particular, concrete being, e.g. an animal, may participate simultaneously in the objective and the subjective mode of being.

[4] From "God's Grandeur" in *The Poems of Gerard Manley Hopkins*, fourth edition (Oxford: Oxford University Press, 1970) p. 66. Hopkins, who knew the classical tradition well, wrote, "I do not think I have ever

simultaneously a power of communication, each being also enjoys a certain availability—which we may call its "signification" or "meaning" (15md.) (Understanding the word "intention" is not absolutely necessary here; cf. the "power of intent" in the following section). As our mortality reminds us, the fact that we have a certain power does not mean that we possess it absolutely. Particular beings have power and autonomy in a real but derivative way, as an instance of "the inclusive and generic power of being to 'communicate' itself" (13). With this recognition, the ghostly notion of a split between objectivity "out there" and subjectivity "in here" begins to dissolve. The terms "subjective" and "objective" need to be understood within the larger context of being and knowing.

II. Being as the Subject of Knowing. Common sense is indeed a mixed bag (19). Sometimes it affords wisdom (e.g. 13md), other times it must be resisted and transcended. In a competitive world of power relationships it can be difficult to conceive of a "power to be affected" (20). We think in terms of acting and being acted upon; it is hard to imagine a third option, a positive power of receptivity. Yet this third way is the key to understanding the act of knowing (20bt).

---

seen anything more beautiful than the bluebell I have been looking at. I know the beauty of our Lord by it" (*The Journals and Papers of Gerard Manley Hopkins*, ed. H. House [London: Oxford University Press, 1959] 199.) The statement can seem unremarkable; but if Hopkins is in earnest, as he seems to be, he is saying that this one tiny, frail flower is more beautiful than, e.g., any sunset he has beheld.

It is hardly too much to say that in the simple act of knowing we show that we can exist outside ourselves, touching the interiority of other beings. Astonishingly, we "grasp immediately and directly" another being's "interior principle of activity" (21md). Here is cause for wonder. The simple act of knowing is a sort of everyday miracle that occurs almost without our realizing it.

The "power of intent" as used in Hartt's text can be puzzling. We may begin by thinking of it as the power of imagination. That conveys the fact that the power of intent is creative (23). But it is misleading insofar as we think of the imagination as being fanciful, whereas the power to intend deals with *meaning* (22bt) or meanings. These have a certain objectivity, as is shown particularly by the realm of formal logic (23tp). Thus the phrase "power of intent" is a useful despite its unfamiliarity because it has a wider scope than "imagination," including "the power to grasp meaning" as well as "the power to express" and create meaning (23md). (A similar point might be made by introducing a hyphen and speaking of the act or event of "mean-ing.")

The act of judging is a further, distinct power of the subject. Again we encounter the power of the subject to transcend itself in the direction of the other. In an act of true judgment, "objective being and subjective being come to be," as it were, "'fused'" (25tp). (Regarding truth we will learn more on page 25.) This quasi-fusion should be associated with the power of "communication" noted earlier. Both terms show how unnecessary it is to fall into the subject-object dichotomy. The problems that arise when one does dichotomize are illustrated with regard to persons at large (25bt) and with regard to God (26).

We have been circling around an utterly extraordinary event of transcendence that is at the same time utterly fundamental. The task of pages 26b-31 is to clarify this event and ground it in being. The abstract character of the discussion is offset by constant reference to two concrete examples, a nose and a dog, and by flashes of humor. Remember that the section is a continuation of the discussion of the power to judge—i.e. of what happens when we try to make a true statement. When we judge, we "attribute" X to Y, e.g. redness to a nose (26bt). In so doing, we initiate a sequence that arrives ultimately at being. As a result of the discussion (the technicalities of which need not be mastered on first reading) the quasi-fusion is grounded in a "juncture" of subjective and objective being that is located in being itself. This juncture is not just true. It is, in effect, truth itself (32).

These formal reflections are important because they provide the basis for the exhilarating affirmation cited earlier, that "all our essentially human appetites" are "satisfied only by being itself" (33). To think that this ultimate term (one might say "reality itself" except that being is even more than "reality") is not hostile or indifferent toward us; that our deepest desires are not absurd delusions but point us toward a goal; and that being itself somehow promises our fulfillment—this is great good news. But, alas, we have trouble receiving it. In *The Romance of the Word*, Robert Farrar Capon describes our historical situation:

> For all the benefits the scientific view brought us, it involved a devastating loss. The medieval universe was a friendly, rational, desiring—and desirable—place. The human beings who inhabited that universe felt at home and even important. . . . The modern universe is not so warm and toasty. It is huge, impersonal, and mute. There is no music of the spheres—only silent, mindless laws. We are not at home in such a universe; we are just insignificant pieces of stuff lost in a crowd of vastly bigger but equally insignificant pieces. After four hundred years we cower like skid-row bums on the doorstep of an indifferent creation. We long for a square meal and a kind word, but we're afraid to believe it when we hear it. Mention a universe run by desire for the Highest Good and, for all our loneliness, we can hardly bring ourselves to trust it.[5]

Capon shows the damage done by "that particular ghost . . . which chatters about the superior reality of the objective over the subjective" (9). At the same time, Capon, who writes these words in the context of a discussion of human suffering, is not naïve. He is aware that in point of fact the world is not always "friendly." But the crucial point is that the medieval worldview is capable of being positive and heartening, even when ill befalls, whereas the modern view is not.

What Hartt is about, for his part, is showing that, contrary to our skid-row skepticism, the underlying truth of the earlier worldview is still available to us. We needn't be intimidated. We can begin to reclaim "a universe run by

---

[5] Robert Farrar Capon, *The Romance of the Word: One Man's Love Affair with Theology* (Grand Rapids: William B. Eerdmans, 1995), 205.

desire for the Highest Good"—provided we step forth to see the world in the light of being.

III. Being as Boundary and as Veil. We are now midway in our reading, with two chapters behind us and two ahead. The first two chapters correspond neatly to the first part of the book's title, *Being Known*; and the final chapter, "Being Unveiled," matches *Being Revealed*. Clearly, the book's project is to forge a connection between being and the God of religious belief, such as existed in classical or premodern thought. But what is the nature of this connection? We will not be far off the mark, I think, if we adopt as our guideline the idea of *mystery* (cf. 35tp). For consider: (1) God is a mystery. Yet (2) God is revealed. What does it mean for a mystery to be revealed? Does it mean that the mystery ceases to be a mystery? One hopes not, for surely that is the broad path leading to bad theology, a god without mystery. But what is the alternative? *How can we think about a mystery that is revealed, yet remains mystery?* If we assume that in the second half of his book Hartt is helping us deal with this difficult but supremely important question, we are likely to keep on track. We can read Chapter III, "Being as Boundary and as Veil," as the place where Hartt sets forth a certain understanding of mystery, which he will then use in Chapter IV

Some of the things we don't know do not deserve the name "mystery"; they reflect "accidental" limitations that may eventually be resolved (35md). Real mystery is "essential": it is not so easily dispelled. It is encountered in both objective (35f.) and subjective (39f.) being. We have already seen (14) that objective being has the power to "act 'from within'" (36), and thus a certain mystery that scientific laws cannot comprehend (36md). But beyond the mystery of objective being lies the truly unsettling mystery, which is that of being itself (36bt). This radical mystery is reflected in the uncertainty of our future (37) and the inscrutability of "the cosmic process" (38). Merely extending life will not give the process meaning (38bt). We bear the weight of an insuperable anxiety (39tp).

Moreover, just as the mystery of being itself lies beyond (the mystery of) objective being, so too it lies beyond subjective being (39md). The result is a "terror" (39bt) which we try to cover over (40). But there is an inevitable return of the repressed; terror denied returns in the guise of "'non-being'" (40md). Popular religion often amounts to another form of the same denial (40bt, 41md). The situation can be described as a sequence of four steps. (i) The collision between being's mystery and our concern for the future causes (ii) a natural anxiety, even terror. (iii) We respond by denial which (iv) only makes things worse. In such a situation, being itself becomes the "enemy" (42md)—albeit only the enemy of our (often religious) delusions.[6]

A more positive side of the veiledness of being itself is that of "solicitation" (41bt) or "summons" (42tp). That call to responsibility bestows a certain purpose or "glory" (43md–bt) in this life. But it is not to be overly personalized

---

[6] The quotation from Capon, offered in reference to Chapters I and II, brings out the pastoral side of Hartt's exposition. With Chapter III the prophetic side becomes more evident.

or sentimentalized, as in much popular religion (42md). The very fact that we hope exposes us to care and failure (42bt–43). Nevertheless, our fragile efforts are given meaning by the awareness that, in and through it all, our deepest desire is "for a disclosure of being itself" (43md).

IV. Being Unveiled. In his treatise *On the Love of God*, Bernard of Clairvaux writes that true religion is a process whereby we begin by loving ourselves for our own sake, then love God but still for our own sake. The crucial turn comes with loving God for God's sake and, Bernard adds in a lovely pastoral touch, loving ourselves for God's sake.[7] Without the conversion to loving God *for God's own sake*, we do not love God but ourselves. We love God for the sake of the rewards God may give us.

One indication of self-love is caring more for particular revealed religious truths (which we take to be the ticket to the reward and the proof of our superiority) than for truth itself. The center of attention and value is still ourselves rather than God; our theology remains anthropocentric. Thinking in terms of "being itself" and "the truth" or "truth itself" will not accomplish the necessary conversion, but it does bear a positive relation to it. It shifts the center away from ourselves, compelling us to think in the most comprehensive terms; and thus it serves as a check against the "false gods" (46md). The terms "being" and "truth" are not interchangeable with "God," but they direct our minds

---

[7] Bernard of Clairvaux, *On Loving God* (Kalamazoo: Cistercian Publications, 1995), 25–30.

toward God. The true God is not less than being, and thus can be loved without holding back—for God's own sake—because in God no aspect of being or truth (or goodness or beauty) is lost.

With this in mind, we can now appreciate the value of speaking of revelation as an event in which the *mystery* of being itself is unveiled by the *power* of being itself (49md). Both terms, mystery and power, are crucial. Earlier we noted that the great problem in thinking about revelation is that it is nearly impossible to think of a mystery as being revealed without its becoming, ipso facto, less mysterious and more obvious. But in revelation there is a power—indeed the revelation is the power—whereby the mystery is unveiled *as mystery*. How is this possible? By a sort of *intensification* (cf. "intensified" 50bt). In revelation there is not simply a meaning (cf. a truth) but an intensification of meaning (49bt). And the intensification relates to the individual person. Revelation is the clarification of the elusive "summons" noted earlier as one of the "veils of being itself" (41bt–42). Revelation clarifies the "inscape" or interiority of the subjective being (cf. 14) in a manner that is uniquely compelling (50md); the power/mystery addresses and enables the person's own "essential power of being" (51md). But it does so without conveying a structure by which the "mortal mind" might, on its own, retrace the way to God (51tp). We attest *that* revelation occurs—but cannot say *how*.

* * *

or sentimentalized, as in much popular religion (42md). The very fact that we hope exposes us to care and failure (42bt–43). Nevertheless, our fragile efforts are given meaning by the awareness that, in and through it all, our deepest desire is "for a disclosure of being itself" (43md).

IV. Being Unveiled. In his treatise *On the Love of God*, Bernard of Clairvaux writes that true religion is a process whereby we begin by loving ourselves for our own sake, then love God but still for our own sake. The crucial turn comes with loving God for God's sake and, Bernard adds in a lovely pastoral touch, loving ourselves for God's sake.[7] Without the conversion to loving God *for God's own sake*, we do not love God but ourselves. We love God for the sake of the rewards God may give us.

One indication of self-love is caring more for particular revealed religious truths (which we take to be the ticket to the reward and the proof of our superiority) than for truth itself. The center of attention and value is still ourselves rather than God; our theology remains anthropocentric. Thinking in terms of "being itself" and "the truth" or "truth itself" will not accomplish the necessary conversion, but it does bear a positive relation to it. It shifts the center away from ourselves, compelling us to think in the most comprehensive terms; and thus it serves as a check against the "false gods" (46md). The terms "being" and "truth" are not interchangeable with "God," but they direct our minds

---

[7] Bernard of Clairvaux, *On Loving God* (Kalamazoo: Cistercian Publications, 1995), 25–30.

toward God. The true God is not less than being, and thus can be loved without holding back—for God's own sake—because in God no aspect of being or truth (or goodness or beauty) is lost.

With this in mind, we can now appreciate the value of speaking of revelation as an event in which the *mystery* of being itself is unveiled by the *power* of being itself (49md). Both terms, mystery and power, are crucial. Earlier we noted that the great problem in thinking about revelation is that it is nearly impossible to think of a mystery as being revealed without its becoming, ipso facto, less mysterious and more obvious. But in revelation there is a power—indeed the revelation is the power—whereby the mystery is unveiled *as mystery*. How is this possible? By a sort of *intensification* (cf. "intensified" 50bt). In revelation there is not simply a meaning (cf. a truth) but an intensification of meaning (49bt). And the intensification relates to the individual person. Revelation is the clarification of the elusive "summons" noted earlier as one of the "veils of being itself" (41bt–42). Revelation clarifies the "inscape" or interiority of the subjective being (cf. 14) in a manner that is uniquely compelling (50md); the power/mystery addresses and enables the person's own "essential power of being" (51md). But it does so without conveying a structure by which the "mortal mind" might, on its own, retrace the way to God (51tp). We attest *that* revelation occurs—but cannot say *how*.

* * *

Julian Hartt has written an autobiography, the title of which, *Yankee Preacher, Prairie Son*, refers jointly to his father and himself. In it he recalls a decisive religious experience that occurred when he was a youth:

> It happened near the end of a simple Sunday evening service. It was a routine occasion, in other words, not the last moments of a salvation campaign. In a quiet and ordinary Sunday evening service . . .
>
> I am not paying particular attention to what the Preacher [his father] is saying because sitting there with Mother I am absorbed by something else, and I am only marginally aware of what this is doing to me. On the blank front wall of the sanctuary a cross is suddenly and unmistakably visible where no cross has ever been displayed. And I hear a voice, certainly not my father's, saying only, "This is for you." The Cross up there for only me to see is empty. And I stand up, certainly without intending or resolving to do so. And I hear my voice saying, "I believe Jesus Christ died for me." And I sit down.[8]

Christian theology has too often approached modern science and culture hat in hand, anxiously inquiring what it might still be able to say. Perhaps the most important thing that I have learned from Julian Hartt is that it does not need to be this way—that there is a depth to the theologian's calling that needn't be intimidated by anything or anyone.[9] The

---

[8] "'What We Make of the World': Excerpts from *Yankee Preacher, Prairie Son*" in *Soundings: An Interdisciplinary Journal*, 81:1–2 (1998), 72.

[9] For example, "It is one thing to say of a scientific theory, It is true.

exuberant breadth of his thinking is one reason Julian em-
bodies this vocation. The unshakeable simplicity of his faith
in Christ is another.[10]

Walter J. Lowe, 2006
Professor of Theology
Emory University

It is quite another to say, Science teaches us what 'true' means." And,
"What the church needs is more chance-taking in the constructive in-
terpretation of its dogmas . . ." (Hartt, just getting started in *A Christian
Critique of American Culture: An Essay in Practical Theology* [New
York: Harper & Row, 1967] 9, 5.)

[10] For more on the relationship of faith, theology and philosophy in
Hartt's thought, see Jonathan R. Wilson, *Theology as Cultural Critique:
The Achievement of Julian Hartt* (Macon: Mercer University Press,
1996).

Julian Hartt has written an autobiography, the title of which, *Yankee Preacher, Prairie Son*, refers jointly to his father and himself. In it he recalls a decisive religious experience that occurred when he was a youth:

> It happened near the end of a simple Sunday evening service. It was a routine occasion, in other words, not the last moments of a salvation campaign. In a quiet and ordinary Sunday evening service . . .
>
> I am not paying particular attention to what the Preacher [his father] is saying because sitting there with Mother I am absorbed by something else, and I am only marginally aware of what this is doing to me. On the blank front wall of the sanctuary a cross is suddenly and unmistakably visible where no cross has ever been displayed. And I hear a voice, certainly not my father's, saying only, "This is for you." The Cross up there for only me to see is empty. And I stand up, certainly without intending or resolving to do so. And I hear my voice saying, "I believe Jesus Christ died for me." And I sit down.[8]

Christian theology has too often approached modern science and culture hat in hand, anxiously inquiring what it might still be able to say. Perhaps the most important thing that I have learned from Julian Hartt is that it does not need to be this way—that there is a depth to the theologian's calling that needn't be intimidated by anything or anyone.[9] The

---

[8] "'What We Make of the World': Excerpts from *Yankee Preacher, Prairie Son*" in *Soundings: An Interdisciplinary Journal*, 81:1–2 (1998), 72.

[9] For example, "It is one thing to say of a scientific theory, It is true.

exuberant breadth of his thinking is one reason Julian em-
bodies this vocation. The unshakeable simplicity of his faith
in Christ is another.[10]

> Walter J. Lowe, 2006
> Professor of Theology
> Emory University

It is quite another to say, Science teaches us what 'true' means." And,
"What the church needs is more chance-taking in the constructive in-
terpretation of its dogmas . . ." (Hartt, just getting started in *A Christian
Critique of American Culture: An Essay in Practical Theology* [New
York: Harper & Row, 1967] 9, 5.)

[10] For more on the relationship of faith, theology and philosophy in
Hartt's thought, see Jonathan R. Wilson, *Theology as Cultural Critique:
The Achievement of Julian Hartt* (Macon: Mercer University Press,
1996).

Preface

Being Known and Being Revealed is the ninth annual Tully Cleon Knoles Lectures in Philosophy. Portions of the Lectures are given orally as part of the annual commencement program. On this occasion selected Junior College educators who are designated as Knoles Fellows discuss the Lectures. For four weeks following commencement the Lectures are critically examined by nationally prominent philosophers at the Pacific Philosophy Institute, which meets at Lake Tahoe. This is done in the vernacular rather than in the technical vocabulary of the philosopher so that persons from many walks of life who attend the Institute—teachers, physicians and nurses, merchants, nuclear physicists, students and housewives—may participate in philosophical discourse.

Julian N. Hartt, the 1957 Knoles Lecturer, is professor of philosophical theology at Yale University. The philosophers for the Philosophy Institute, which is in its tenth year, include: Swami Akhilananda (Massachusetts Ramakrishna-Vedanta Society); Edwin Ding (College of the Pacific); Arturo Fallico (San Jose State); James L. Hagerty (St. Mary's College, California); Paul Holmer, (University of Minnesota); William P. Kent (University of Utah); John F. Lawry (College of the Pacific); Gordon F. Matheson (University of Southern California); Daniel L. McGloin, S.J. (Loyola University, Los Angeles); Patrick Romanell (University of Texas); Alan Watts (American Academy of Asian Studies of the College of the Pacific); Donald A. Wells (State College of Washington). William D. Nietmann, College of the Pacific, is Director of the Institute.

The following distinguished Junior College educators, who represent many academic fields, constitute the 1957 class of Knoles Fellows: Milton Black (Shasta); Harold E. Chastain (Sierra); Donald Ericksen (Reedley); John Fannuchi (Stockton); Don O. Howard (Bakersfield); Eleanor Maderis (San Jose); Glenn C. Martin (Santa Monica); Everett F. McCartney (Vallejo); Catherine Clara Patterson (Sacramento); E. J. Portugal (Santa Rosa); N. Arthur Rasmuson (Glendale); J. Kenneth Rowland (Modesto); Leslie E. Wilbur (Bakersfield); Richard Worthen (East Contra Costa).

Stockton, California

March 30, 1957

CONTENTS

BEING AS THE OBJECT OF KNOWLEDGE

THE TITLE OF THE BOOK states its theme, for in it we discuss certain aspects of the problem, "What Can Be Known About Reality?" I have not approached this problem by way of enumerating and classifying the kinds of entities and events disclosed in human knowledge; and little attention has been given to standard epistemological questions, such as, how do we know, how is perception related to "the external world" on the one hand and to the other powers of the mind on the other hand, etc. These questions are probably important, but I believe that certain questions about being have a natural priority relative to them. Furthermore, a law of diminishing returns has long since been in evidence in the field of discourse called "philosophy of religion," and especially in those sub-regions of that area called "the problem of religious knowledge." There thinkers peer earnestly into nets of knowing used to catch ordinary and natural things of experience, to see whether they can identify any object properly divine. But the nets may not be right for "divine objects," and, for that matter, they may not be entirely right for anything else, either. The thinker ought not to be hasty, then, in deciding that Deity is beyond all our knowing, if Deity exists at all. It is possible that Deity does not adjust itself to our ordinary schemes of knowing but is nonetheless truly divine. And there is the further possibility that Deity is self-certified as immediately present to the awareness of the creature in such a way as to constitute a "knowing beyond knowing." If this were so, it would make hash out of any effort to make the schemes of ordinary knowing all-comprehensive by definition. But this does not mean that "revelation," so understood, bears no identifiable relations to the structures of knowing. Indeed, it is one of our theses in these lectures that the revelation of God *does* exhibit identifiable relations to the structures of knowing.

Nothing is farther from our intent than to propose that religious people really must believe something they don't believe or that they ought not to believe something they do believe. And I do not want to suggest, either, that only one scheme of interpretation for the "facts of revelation" is forthcoming, and that reasonable people ought to settle for it promptly. The intent is to open up questions. We do not want to encapsulate God and the World in a glass tomb. Our program is less ambitious than that. Whether or not the things people say about God are true, their utterances do exhibit certain meanings and patterns of meaning. Specifically, many of the things said about God by religious people presuppose things about being itself and about being as known. We shall move in this "back-world" of things presupposed in much religious discourse. And this requires a certain kind of self-abnegation, perhaps several kinds. For one thing the question of the truth of religious teachings about God will have to be temporarily suspended; for another, we shall have to contain our enthusiasm and our natural preference for the rich poetic ranges of religious expression. The concrete fullness of religious thought and feeling cannot be found in the "back-worlds" of our investigation, and we shall gain nothing from trying to pack that richness into that relatively arid country.

Our order of procedure is as follows. *Being Known* is discussed in the first two lectures. *Being Revealed* is the theme of lectures Three and Four.

The Notion of Being

The subject of our enquiry is *being* rather than *reality*. The reasons for putting being in the primary position can be quickly suggested, even though we do not elaborate them here in any detail. For one thing, being is the more inclusive term, since "unreal" things have *some* kind of being. Too, "reality" is a term loaded with value-judgment. Fortunately, we have not yet done this to the term "being." When a person says "this is reality," we expect him to sigh blissfully or to burst into song. It isn't easy to put the same kind of flavor into the term "being."[1] Finally, if we begin from being, we may hope to be liberated along the line from certain ghosts that haunt the distinction between subjective and objective being; and from that particular ghost, persuasive enough yet to retain a sizeable company of true believers, which chatters about the superior reality of the objective over the subjective.

But if being is the first object of our attention, what is being? If it turns out that being is the broadest of all possible notions, everything said about being would have to be said in terms of being. But this should not prevent our being able to say, at least in a loose way, what we are talking about when we are talking about

---

1. Though no advance preparation is likely to be very helpful in arming one against the day, we may expect sooner or later to hear: "man, that has being!" In the meantime, we ought to be patient under "that is for real" and suffer in quietness of mind when a vocalist bellows praise of "Reality!"

being. What, then, are we saying when we say that being is the broadest of all basic terms of discourse? The statement means that every particular thing has and exhibits a kind of unity with all other things: they are all things *of* something and things *about* something which itself is not exhausted in any particular thing nor in any series or collection of particular things.[2] Moreover, when we say that a particular thing has being, we generally mean that it is *actual*. But actuality is only one of the modes of being. Another mode is already indicated by the subject of the proposition, "Something is actual." In other words, *to be* has a meaning distinct from *to be actual*. *To be* stands over against non-being, that is, against not-to-be. *Not-to-be* does not mean simply failure to be actual, for so far as something can be just thought it has a kind of being, whether or not it is concretely actual, a member of some state of affairs or "world."

Since *to be* seems to require *not-to-be*, does this mean that non-being shares priority with being itself? Non-being is a fundamental notion, however odd it looks in common-sense discourse, but being does not share its primacy with non-being. Further on we shall see how *non-being* presupposes the undistributed primacy of being.

Being cannot be properly defined, but this does not mean that we cannot know being. Everything known (whether actual or

---

2. **World** must be distinguished from **Being**. It is well to use **world** to signify "the system of things in general," which includes both actual things and possible things (things that can be consistently conceived as available for actualization in the given world). From this alone it is clear that **being** is a broader notion than **world**: there are ways of being which have nothing to do with schemes of actualization.

merely conceivable) is known as being and as some particular form or mode of being.

Objective Being as the Power to Appear

The discovery of being does not seem to be either a very exciting or a very important affair. We may feel that we could live without having made this discovery of being. Perhaps we feel this way because we seem to have a greater natural interest in discovering the kinds of being and especially the kinds of being that are "more real" than others. This natural interest may not be quite as common or quite as exclusive as it seems. And it may be "natural" *for us* because a certain doctrine about being has been proclaimed so long and so passionately that we have little enthusiasm for questioning it. I mean the doctrine of the greater reality of objective being.[3] Whether or not the doctrine is sound (and we ought to raise this question), we would do well to overcome any slavish adherance to it. One way of attempting to achieve this kind of free attitude toward the doctrine is to consider *objective* and *subjective* as ways of being.

What is objective being? Something is an "object" when we can attend to it with a sound expectation that the act of attending

---

3. Ordinary discourse is confused about and by this doctrine. Sometimes we feel that "objective reality" is certainly more important than "subjective reality"; but what about the times when we feel that our **feelings** are more important than the "objective facts"? Then we are prepared either to fly in the face of the "facts," or to poke around to find the facts that will substantiate our feelings. And there are moments in which we express troubled reservations about "objectivity" as a suitable attitude with which to approach certain "realities," e.g., a love-affair.

to it will not seriously alter or corrupt its true character. Thus to be an object something must have a certain *thereness* about it. Suppose I say, "There is the pretty girl I was talking about last night." You say, "Where?" (Of course you could say something else, such as, "Do you call her pretty?"). I reply, "There." If she isn't looking in our direction, I point to her, in order to direct your attention to the proper (we hope) object. The object is not merely in my head— if she were, I couldn't point her out. She is *there*. We may not agree that she is pretty, but our disagreement about this does not affect her being there. She may leave that particular place if she overhears us arguing about her prettiness, but she will not lose her objective being simply because we do not agree on her beauty. Even if our quarrel upset her so badly that she committed suicide she would not thereby lose all her objective being, though we do not know whether what was left to her after that desperate act would do her or us much good.

So far, then, we say that for something to be an object it must have a certain power of being: *it must be able to appear to another being, in such a way as to show or communicate something true of itself.* "Common Sense" seems to express a greater interest in the knowing subject and its powers than in the powers of the object, but common-sense shows here how it has been corrupted by philosophical traditions. We are tempted to say, for instance, that the objects of human knowledge are mere "appearances" of things whose "real" being we have no access to. But these "appearances" are either created by the knower, by presumptive powers in him of which he has no direct knowledge at all; or by the object-thing in or behind the "appearance." Here Common Sense holds that appearances are more or less reliable manifestations of objective things; and that objective things are always giving off these manifestations whether knowers are around to receive them or not; for if "appearances" are special efforts on the part of things, put forward to impress beings with power to know, the presence of the knower *does* make a difference to the thing known, and objective being has lost something of its objectivity. For the purposes of common-sense dealings with the world, and also for some of the purposes of science, we should like to have things simply be themselves in our knowledge of them: we are not at all sure that we can trust something which goes out of its way to impress us. And here Common Sense is on the right track. Power to appear is a natural power in things and we have not the slightest reason to suppose that the exercise of this power falsifies the nature of the thing at all. To put the matter positively, *power to appear is one aspect or form of the inclusive and generic power of being to "communicate" itself*. Communication, so understood, is the pattern or patterns a thing has in relation to other things in which its true nature is exhibited. Communication to a mind is one form of this. Communication to a being without mind is something else: the difference one molecule makes to another, and to all others, is its "communication" of itself to things which do not appear to have "minds." This is a way of saying that all things are in transaction and that knowing is one kind of transaction. We may make knowing as special as we want or feel we must, up to the point where we suppose that the thing known is essentially different from the thing itself. Beyond that point "knowing" ceases to be a meaningful transaction with being beyond the knower.

Objective Being as the Power to Act from Interior Principle

Another feature of objective being is the *power to act from interior principle*. When we are dealing with an objective thing we know that we are dealing with something which has its own source of activity within itself, at least relative to the knower. We know also that this source is concealed from us: its power to act is "interior" to itself. We know what it is specifically only so far as it "appears." Generically, we know something about it, as we are now seeing. But the concrete objective entity has its principle of activity to itself and in itself, as far as it is truly concrete and truly individual. This interior principle of activity is not known directly. Moreover, for certain purposes we can pretend that there is no such principle in objective beings. The things we make, for instance, have a certain kind of objectivity—you can fall over a rake and break a leg, and you could not do this if the rake weren't really there and if the leg weren't there, too; but we can use a rake in any purpose for which it will serve without wondering about its "soul." Naturally a rake has its limitations, and these express and define its nature. The rake is yours, you may even have made it, but even so it has a kind of life to itself, so far as your being able to do anything about it. You can rake with it, but you can't water the tomato plants with it, and you can't mount it and sail away, over spire and over glen, to some witches' rendezvous.[4] The limitations of the rake are derived finally not from some defect in

---

4. Folk-lore and fairy-land are richly populated with runaway utensils seeking and finding redress and revenge for years of dumb submission. The folk-lore of our technological culture has its own nightmares, in which the Machine devours the mechanic.

the imagination and mechanical aptitude of the inventor and wielder of the tool, but from the nature of the material used in the tool. The elementary components of this material act from their own centers and not in obedience to our wills and minds.

Objective Being as the Power to Be Signified

Objective being has a further feature which deserves our attention: *it is that which is intended in our knowledge and discourse: it is what we mean.* And here we must say something about intention and meaning.

Intention is the signification of a word (or non-verbal gesture), where "signification" is not simply another word but a state of affairs or some component of a state of affairs. Thus intention is *being signified.* Intention so understood is not the same as purpose or intent. (Purpose and intent have to do with being as subject, and we shall have something to say about them under that heading in Lecture Two.)

The "meaning" of meaning is objective being. When we say that something is the meaning of a statement or expression, we are dealing with objective being as that which can be attended to as having a certain character or nature. Even when we say that the meaning of a line of poetry is an emotion or a feeling, we do not suppose that the emotion meant is so elusive and unreal that no statement of it and about it could conceivably be true. The richness of the emotion is certainly not captured in the line of poetry; but the emotion *is* there in a certain mode, and specifically, in the objective mode.

We are not proposing that objective being is all of being. We are saying that being as such has an objective mode; and that every particular being and every occurrence of being, has its objective aspect. Everything can be expressed, in one way or another. All being admits signification, either concretely or abstractly. We must note, however, that our finite minds cannot match the power of signification in being itself. There are indeed more things in heaven and earth than we can dream of: but we know something in the abstract about all of them. We cannot do much with them or about them in that form, to be sure, but we have enough to keep us busy, though not so much that we cannot in good faith yearn for more.

"Internal" and "External"

Objective being has been set forth as having these powers: to appear, to act from interior principle, to be signified. We find now that we cannot postpone conscientiously coping with a question asked out of philosophic prejudice: don't we normally think of objective being as being "external" to the knower, being that is "out there" rather than "in here'"? Very likely. And this *is* a prejudice. "External" and "internal" are very rough distinctions at best, whatever their everyday usefulness. Surely the sensation of hardness to touch is as "internal," considered just as sensation, as the sensation of sweetness to taste or smell; and neither is more or less "internal" than a sensation of hunger or a feeling of loneliness. Everyday dealings with the "natural" world are manageable on the loose assumption that sun and moon and falling bodies are not moved by either hunger or loneliness; and that beauty is only in the eye of the beholder. Yet if everyday dealings exhausted our interests, and answered the questions the "natural" world itself begets in us, we should have no need of philosophy or of religion or art. We conclude that "external" and "internal" are only what they appear to be, rough-and-ready distinctions useful for everyday dealings with the world. They do not say much about being; they do not even say very much about "reality."

A singular virtue nevertheless abides in the common-place distinction between external and internal and in the correlative prejudice concerning the superior reality of the external. That virtue is revealed in the conviction that objective being is or contains the ultimate criteria of truth in knowing. A statement is true just so far as evidence is available that things really are as the statement declares them to be. We can indeed make up our minds to believe that a statement must be true—we do this everyday and part of the time we get away with it; but unless being objectively certifies itself to us as conforming to that belief, we are marked for madness.

We shall not be in a sound position from which to see how objective being functions as prime criterion of knowledge until we have considered as carefully as we can the prime features of being as the subject of knowing, to which we turn.

BEING AS THE SUBJECT OF KNOWING

T HE WORLD OF COMMON SENSE is made up of objects and subjects, things known and knowers, and in that world some objects are also knowers or subjects, and some are not; and beyond that world there are things which are not objects ("unknown things"), and knowers of far greater power than we ("God", "angels", "Martian minds", etc.). As usual, the world of common-sense is a glorious hodge-podge of fact and fancy, held together by low-grade utility, and endurable to thought only as grist for its mill.

Objective and subjective are most meaningful distinctions when they are first related to being itself[1] rather than to presumptively different kinds of entities between which a presumptive relation called knowledge is then spun out of largely practical necessities.

Subjective being signifies different but related modes of being: (1) being as the knowing agent, (2) being as the subject of all attributions. Since we are more generally familiar with the first signification as the proper one for "subjective being" we shall start

---

1. As we use the term **being itself,** it does not signify a substantial individual being of any sort or any kind of entity. No single entity, and no state of affairs, is the sole and proper denotation of the term **being.** In this respect, and in others, **being itself** is simply an emphatic way of writing **being.** The force of **itself,** thus, is merely to emphasize that we are not referring to any particular being. **Being as such** is another phrase used for this same purpose.

19

there, and then proceed to the second mode. Ideally, this procedure will bring us to the point where we can grasp the "juncture"
of the objective and the subjective modes of being.

Subjective Being as the Power to be Affected

Subjective being[2] is being as knowing and knower. What are
the distinctive powers of such being? We see at once that subjective
being is the *power to be affected*. *To be affected* is not the same as
to be effected. An effect is a determination of a determinate cause.
An affect is a modification of a being induced in it either by that
being itself or by another being. For example, a sensitive person is
affected by the suffering of another, but this does not mean that his
sympathy is a mere effect of an external cause. His feelings are
aroused by his perception of the other person's pain; but his own
power of being may be just as truly expressed in his sympathy as
the power of another. Where this is not the case one suspects
that another is "playing on his feelings," that is, that someone is
trying to make him an *effect*.

Now knowing is plainly an affective relation and activity, at
every important level or degree of knowledge. Knowledge of con-
ceptual and purely formal abstractions involves the lowest degree
of affectedness. "Existential knowledge" involves the highest and

---

2. We break with Common-Sense so far as it is committed
to an hard-and-fast distinction between "subjective world" and
"objective world." In this view one's personal feelings etc. constitute a private realm of being set over against a public realm
of fact, things everybody can see for himself, scientific entities,
etc. Certainly there is "privacy" and there is much we can talk
about on the practically warranted assumption that it is "out
there" for everybody. But we have no good reason for making
two "worlds" out of these respective kinds of experience.

richest degree of affectedness. In between are many shades and blends, but all knowing exhibits some degree and kind of affectedness.

Knowing is not the only form of affectivity in subjective being. Significant (perhaps all) relations of one being to another presuppose affectivity in the subject of the relations. Further attention to this, again, is reserved for being as the subject of all attributions.

Subjective Being as the Power to Grasp an Interior Principle of Activity

Subjective being, secondly, has *the power to grasp immediately an interior principle of activity*.

If we supposed that this power to grasp immediately and directly an interior principle of activity was the same as self-consciousness, we should have made our own psychological make-up very nearly the whole meaning of subjective being in the first mode. We do not want to do this. Whatever manifests and persists in a pattern of activity, has this grasp; so that direct awareness of this principle of activity, such as we do have in ourselves, is not the only form of this "grasp". My collie dog Prince has a form of it, even though he is not terribly bright. I identify him by a combination of his appearance and his behavior—the way he looks and the way he acts (badly, most of the time). But he does not need to correlate his own appearance and his own behavior to be himself. His being Prince is patterned from within, his activities are determined by the internal principle of his own nature.

Self-consciousness is a certain dimension, and perhaps we might also say a certain perfection, of this power. It does not follow from this, however, that a person (a self-conscious subject) has his nature simply or primarily from the act of self-awareness. The correctness and truth of this implication depends entirely on whether we are thinking of self-awareness as an activity or as an end-product, that is, of what a person is aware of when he is self-conscious. The activity pertains to the very essence, so to say, of the person; but what he is aware of in self-consciousness may easily be a more or less incidental detail of his existence. Being aware of oneself is a process or activity in which many details and elements of one's being may be pulled together into the kind of unity we mean by the term *person* or *personhood*. Indeed, being a person is impossible without self-awareness. A human being may have other kinds of unity, to be sure, and some of these are not conspicuously different in complexity or nobility from what can be seen in my dog Prince.

Subjective Being as the Power of Intent

A third feature of subjective being as knower is *the power to intend*. Just as objective being has the power to be intended, so subjective being has the power to express and to grasp intentions (meanings). When we are thinking about the "external" world of sense-perception, we interpret this power of intending as being able to read the appearances of natural objects, not infallibly, but yet with practically satisfying results. Sense-perception is being affected; but sense-perception is *knowing* only when the meaning of the perception-event is grasped and is assimilated to a pattern of meanings.

Relative to other realms of objective being beyond the realm of sense-perception, the same thing must be said, with suitable modifications derived from the character of the realm of being considered. Take, for example, the realm of pure logic. It is not sullied by any mere matter of fact. Being is allowed here only so far as it has surrendered any claim to truth and is willing to survive on a diet of pure validity. The principle holds here, nonetheless, with undiminished force: knowing is the power to grasp intentions. In this case nothing is "projected" upon other being, as in the instance of sense-perception. The meanings are not attributed to anything other than themselves—we cannot conclude from them to the world of "fact"; they have their being in themselves.[3]

The power to intend is not merely the power to grasp meanings, it is also the power to *express* meanings. *Creative* is an adjective properly to be thought of in this connection, since the higher ranges of subjective being show greater and greater creativity of intention. It may seem playful to remark that the nervous system in the higher animals, and certainly in man, is a kind of biological poet, because it persistently puts more meaning into its world than it has gotten out of it, and such is essentially the work of poetry. Nevertheless the observation has a serious side to it, as well as truth somewhere in it. Personal being is creative. In ourselves, this creative power requires a supply of material submitted to us from beyond us; but it is quite a serious mistake to say that man is creative

---

3. And thereby hangs many and many a tale of piteous philosophical and even theological disaster, tales of how noble minds were seduced by the infertile virginity of pure logical essences into supposing that ultimate perfection of being would somehow partake of this quality of being. Of a truth, this is a realm into which thief or moth or rust does not intrude; but nothing can happen there, good or bad.

only in the re-arrangements effected in the given materials. Novelty, real rather than merely psychological, is within our grasp: an authentic person is subjective being enriched and enriching beyond the bare allowances of given nature. Thus the power to intend is a prime power of subjective being.

Subjective Being as the Power to Judge

A fourth power of subjective being as knowing and knower is *the power to judge*. In the human subject (the person) judging or the act of judgment is the culminative phase of the process of knowing. This act assimilates the presentational content (a sense-datum, a memory-image or what-not) to a structure of meanings, and thus ushers the mind of the knower into the "declaratory mood": he is prepared to say what the thing is that is being presented in his act of awareness. Only when the knower has entered the declaratory mood is he (or anyone else) able to test the judgment. The tests are varied. In some instances the first test is, Do the facts confirm the judgment? Another test of judgment is suggested by the question, Does the proposition really follow from other propositions, as the judgment declares? But whatever the test or the modification of the test employed, the act of judging is also apparent in the test of judgment, which is suggested in the common-sense observation that the amount of evidence necessary to confirm a judgment about fact is itself a "matter of judgment."

Judgment (judging) ought not to be so interpreted that the distinction between knowing and knowing the truth is blurred. (Other things contribute to this unfortunate effect.) Knowing as such is a transaction within being, first of all; and, more specifically, it is a process in which objective being and subjective being come to be related in a certain way—"fused," we are tempted to say—in the subjective act of judgment. Knowing the truth, on the other hand, is the process in being itself which transcends the distinction between objective being and subjective being; which is to say that "truth" is a name of being itself and not for a mode of being. We all know, of course, that "truth" is commonly used in trivial ways, both in ordinary discourse and in more refined speech such as science and philosophy. It is said, e.g., that truth is a function of propositions, that it is a peculiar kind of agreement of ideas in the head with the world outside the head, etc. These are ways (and there are others) in which truth is made a property of mind or mental being; yet they all use this property called "truth" in some way or other to relate subjective being to objective being. We find it necessary not to stop there, and presently we shall see why and how this is so.

Before we consider subjective being as the subject of all attributions we ought to ponder what kind of seriousness is to be found in the view that subjective being cannot be known as such, since whatever is *known* is so far objective. As a protest against defective accounts of objective being, this view deserves to be taken seriously. As an account of subjective being the view itself is defective and ought to be suitably emended, since it assumes that a particular being, such as a person, is either objective or subjective being, or is more largely or "ultimately" the one rather than the other. Such assumptions have little merit beyond run-of-the-mill utility. Every subject-being has its objective side: objective being derives its activity and its character from an interior source—the "secret" of its being is not disclosed in its appearances: its appearances are at once a showing-forth, and a concealment.

We also hear a good deal from theological quarters today about the "distorting" effect of our knowing objective being; and, specifically, about the emptiness of any claim to knowledge of God, on the grounds that God is Subject and cannot be object. Here again we detect defective views of subjective and objective. The mind "distorts" what it knows only in the sense that it seeks to assimilate presentational events, so far as they have meaning, into structures of meaning. But since objective being has the power to be intended, that is, to "become a meaning," "distortion" is not a serious problem unless the process of assimilation destroys or subverts the meaning communicated in the presentational event. Undoubtedly this happens. But why should we suppose that "God" is the pure and simple case of such error? So far as God is being or has being, He has pre-eminently the power to "become a meaning." We say in all confidence that God is more than a meaning, but we say this, in this context, because God has in himself all the powers of being, subjective and objective.

Being Itself as the Ultimate Subject of Attribution

In the beginning of this chapter we proposed to consider as the second mode of subjective being, *being as the subject of all attributions*. Turning to this, we first ask about *attribution* itself. Attribution does not seem to be a very mysterious matter. "John's nose is red"—red is attributed to the nose, and, by the use of the possessive, the nose to John. Accordingly "nose" is the nearer subject of attribution, and "John" is the further and more inclusive subject of attribution, since the nose is a feature of John and John is not a feature of the nose (except in special cases). But the first question about attribution arises right here: what prevents us logically from saying that beyond every nearer subject of attribution and every relatively further one ("John" in the example above), there is one all-inclusive subject of attribution, *being itself*? A second question follows immediately from the first: Do we say anything important in saying this about being itself even if logically we were compelled to say it?

In dealing with the first question we find it necessary again to note that everything attributed has some kind and degree of being. But something must be added to this principle. Everything attributed (to whatever subject, with one exception) "belongs" first to *being* rather than to the particular subject to which it is assigned in the judgment of attribution. Consider again John's red nose. The redness of John's nose is not simply dependent for being upon that nose, or upon any nose, or upon any particular concrete entity anywhere or anytime. Furthermore, the nose contributes nothing distinctive to redness as such, unless one wishes to say, somewhat playfully, that you never knew what red could be until you saw John's nose.

And shall we not say the same, in principle, about the relation of the nose to John? Yes, perhaps with some certain distinctions. Again we can say that John gains distinctiveness by virtue of his nose, rather than the nose from its presence on John's face. A certain amount of playfulness is apparent in this formulation, to be sure, since noses in fact are always on faces and are always of faces (barring ghastly accidents, of course); and even abstractly you cannot successfully separate the meaning of "nose" from the meaning of "face." But it is not whimsical to say that "nose" has a certain meaning and as such a certain status in being quite independent of "John" and, indeed, of all smelling creatures. Even if you imagined that all smelling creatures had vanished from the the universe; or that smelling creatures had not yet appeared in the actual universe; in either case "nose", an instrument for smelling, is yet a possibility, and a possibility which in no way depends upon "John" or any other conceivable creature.

In the *actual* world however, features of things do depend upon the things of which they are features—actual noses are parts of faces, actual colors are qualities of noses, etc. But are the "further" subjects of ordinary discourse—John and the maple tree and Arcturus and Prince—properly to be treated as "features" or qualities of *being itself,* the all-inclusive and ultimate subject of attribution? If so, beings we judge to be "real" subjects, such as ourselves, would seem to dissolve into "aspects" of Being, a result acutely dissatisfying to many people who say that they don't *feel* like "aspects," and accordingly do not want other people telling them they really are anyway. Philosophical decision of the first importance cannot be made simply by appeals to "feeling", certainly; but these decisions cannot be adequately made, either, in bland indifference to the fact that "feelings" of this order are sometimes poorly-expressed intuitions of undeniable realities. So, the feeling of undeniable and irreducible reality in ourselves as subjects (persons), has a right to be heard and a right to make itself as clear as possible.

At this point we want to be clear, too, about attribution. Attribution treats all beings indifferently, so far as they fall within its rules at all. And the basic rule is: *the relation between predicates and subjects is asymmetrical,* that is, if *x* can be predicated of *A, A* as such cannot be predicated of *x* (except playfully, "redness is nosed in John", "nose is Johned", etc.) It may be that *A* is only a grammatical subject and that *A* can be predicated of something else, but this is not an exception to the rule.[4] If *A* is a real subject, then *A* cannot be predicated of anything else. The predicates of *A* relate *A* to other real subjects in some instances—if *A* is married he is married to someone (or was—the question of change of marital status is not decisive here, whatever it may have actually done to *A*.) But when *A's* predicates are relational in this sense, they do not diminish his subject-hood.

Is the first rule of attribution violated, then, when we say that being itself is the ultimate subject of all attribution? It is not. The proposition, *being itself is the ultimate subject of all attribution,* means that everything particular, whether it is a property, an aspect, or a real subject, "participates" in being, and that being itself cannot be said to participate in particular things etc., in the same way. "Redness" participates in being in several different ways; being does not participate in redness. The modes of participation in being are infinitely diverse but in no case can we say seriously that being itself participates in the mode.

Since there are real subjects, it follows that they participate

---

4. The rule is not in the first instance a rule of syntax or of Indo-European grammatical structures. We are dealing in this rule with an expression of an **intuition of being.** The intuited **subject** is a center of power. Its activities evince the properties attributed to it and thus we can say that it "organizes its predicates around itself."

in being as real subjects rather than as properties or aspects. In this sense real subjects can be attributed to being itself without jeopardizing their status in being. And if real subjects have qualities which as such relate them to being itself as subject, these qualities cannot entail a diminution in their real subject-hood. Whether there are such relational qualities in real subjects is a question we must presently consider. But before we turn to that, let us try to make good on the claim that being as the subject of all attribution is the only basis upon which the "juncture" of objective being and subjective being can be adequately grasped; the juncture being the "realm" of truth.

Truth as the "Juncture" of Subjective and Objective Being

Being itself is the ultimate intention of every proposition for which a claim as true can be made, for when we assert that a proposition is true we are asserting that the "plan of attribution" exhibited in the proposition is a faithful exemplification of being itself. When we say that proposition x is true, we do not mean that something like it is true, or that it holds good somehow or other for the "real world." If that is what we mean when we claim truth for proposition x, then we ought to find some word to use in place of "truth." [5]

A proposition is a "plan of attribution" because its intent is to identify correctly and to relate correctly subjective being in a

---

5. The substitution has long since become routine in some quarters, e.g., in scientific discussion where propositions are said to be probable in some degree; and in some theological discussion, where propositions are said to be "true for the true believer" and not true as such.

certain mode to objective being in a certain mode or modes. A simple illustration comes to mind: *Prince did not kill your chickens.* The obvious elements in this statement can be quickly enumerated:

(1) Your chickens are dead and were obviously killed;

(2) You (or someone whose judgment you rate as highly as you do your own) saw Prince near your chicken-house; perhaps with chicken-feathers in his mouth;

(3) I have good (and I think sufficient) reason for denying that Prince is the culprit, e.g., I may believe that he doesn't like chicken; or he was in the hospital at the time of the crime, recovering from his having eaten your neighbor's chickens.

In these elements subjective being is involved at several points (*subjective,* not psychological). Prince is a subject of predications, obviously, but here *we* are too, trying to discern the true meaning amid the (objective) appearances. The objective appearances include not only Prince's visible behavior but also the things you and I do which are occasion for interpretation to the other. I do not *know* that Prince is the kind of being metaphysically incapable of eating your chickens, though I do know that there are such beings. And I do not *know* that you really don't believe your accusation against Prince is true but are trying to embarrass me to the point where I shall feel I must leave the community. No, the proposition, *Prince did not kill your chickens,* is true, not by virtue of things unknown and unknowable, but by virtue of things known, i.e., so far as it rightly relates appearances to subjects, and, therefore, only so far as *power to be intended* is matched by the *power to intend.*

We say then that the truth of a proposition is more than finding out that what it says is so: a proposition is true only when we find out that being is as the proposition claimed it to be. If we find out that something like the proposition is true, no particular honor is bestowed on that particular propostion. And the broadly popular notion that many true propositions nonetheless need revision in the light of new knowledge etc., is a very seductive error. "The sun moves, the earth stands still" is as true today as it ever was, if by "sun" you mean a particular appearance and by "earth" the solid affair we walk upon. "The sun moves, etc.," *does* exhibit a "plan of attribution" between appearances confirmed by the appearances alone, beyond the shadow of a doubt.

Since every proposition is a scheme of attribution, we infer from this that every scheme of attribution is a structure of being itself. But this means only that being itself is the *intention* of every such structure. The structure may falsify, concretely or factually. *Only where the structures of attribution manifest the intention of being itself, is truth signified.*

Truth, then, pertains to being itself rather than either to objective being or subjective being. That is why we say that truth lies at the juncture of objective and subjective being, and that it is neither the property of "minds" or of "things" considered in abstraction from being.

Being as the subject of all attribution might well be called the prime mode of subjective being. *Being* represents itself both in infinitely diverse particular things and events, and in the modes, subjective and objective. (There are other modes which we have arbitrarily excluded from detailed consideration here). We lack the concrete intuition of *being itself*. Because we lack this we find it very easy to set the idea of being very far down the list of important terms, and sometimes assign it a purely verbal and grammatical quality. This is a monumental error. The appetite of the mind we call "knowing" is an appetite satisfied only by being itself; and what holds for mind, holds for all our essentially human appetites. What we cannot live without is no mere affair of grammar.

BEING AS BOUNDARY AND AS VEIL

Every account of being as known must reckon with the boundaries of knowledge and with the mystery of being itself. The boundaries are of two kinds, the temporal and accidental on the one hand, and the essential and insurmountable on the other hand. The mystery of being itself is manifested in the essential and insurmountable boundaries of knowledge, which we shall treat as the veil of being. But the mystery of being is also manifest in the unveiling of being, which is our subject in the fourth lecture.

Objective Being and the Meaning of Existence

Temporal and accidental limitations of knowledge are encountered at many points in objective being. Old appearances, so to speak, must be correlated with new appearances, according to certain rules of human devising which are nonetheless (in some cases) so beautiful and so fertile for further investigation that we call them "laws of nature". And we have every reason to believe that other things will appear to upset even the most venerable rules now stock-in-trade in the sciences. But we don't know when this will happen or what they will be.

Objective being sets more enduring boundaries against our knowledge, and these we call *essential* simply because they pertain to the very nature of objective being. The interior principle of

35

activity in objective beings is not known to us, except in very general terms. Molecules, we hear, are electricity. Does this mean anything more than that "molecule" stands for an occurrence on a complex measuring device? Or does it mean that the "molecule" is a structure of being, a pattern or a member of a pattern of actual events? Fools rush in etc., but we refuse to be tempted beyond our strength. Whatever we say in general molecules *really* are, individual molecules (if there are any such actual entities), act "from within" and not as externally determined effects of "laws". And the closer we come to the concrete world of our experience, the clearer it becomes to us that objective being, now as in other persons, "conceals" the interior principle of activity. Here especially, "predictability" does *not* mean that the predictor has grasped the interior center of activity. Activity assumes pattern: and prediction is a matter of betting on a manifest pattern, that it will be sustained into the future (into the "calculable future", that is).

The center of interior activity is not the only being veiled by being itself. Being itself turns a blank face to our questions, Why? and Whither? Being known and being knowing, is a world of meaning. There meanings abound, more than we can adequately assimilate, more than we rightly grasp and comprehend. But we cannot add these meanings together in such a way as to solve the riddle of existence, whether it be our existence or the existence of anything that in fact exists. True, we have recourse to attitudes calculated to soothe the spirit under the stress of the riddle of existence. To the child who asks, "Why do I exist", we administer one or a combination of the tranquilizers: "the stork brought you"; "Daddy fertilized Mummy at just the right time"; *"your* life-story begins millions of years ago"; "God dreamed you in order to make Mummy and Daddy happy" etc. ad naus. Apparently our pious hope is that if the child's instinctive hunger for truth of being (for which "curiosity" is much too slack a word) is deadened systematically with such formulae, such bottled pap, he will eventually become easy to live with, i.e., he will become mature. But the achievement is at best precarious. We know ourselves as beings whose prime actions are governed by ends—we act, upon those occasions in which our proper selfhood and humanity are evidenced, on purpose, and have every day to answer to self and to others, the question, *Why?* And so also for *Whither?* We cannot help ourselves, we are inwardly compelled to ask about the future, about our own future—whatever our philosophical disagreements over Time, we live by thought of the future. Who strikes *Destiny* from his account of human existence, is self-blinded, out of recklessness, ignorance, or fear.

Why? and Whither? haunt our existence, and we cannot refrain from putting the questions to all that is and to the depths of being from which all have come forth. But being itself does not answer these questions. Whatever exists might not have existed. Odd as it may seem, we have a more reasonable account of why much that exists should cease sometime to exist, than we do of why *anything* should exist. This does not mean that we have an old grudge against existence, not at all (though indeed some appear to); fundamentally it means that no being bears within it an adequate reason for its presence in the scheme of things entire.— And again, *Whither?* "Brethren, it does not yet appear what we shall become", so runs Scripture. And to this we must add, it appears even less what other things are to become, or what the scheme of things is to be. A deep religious faith cries out (in litanies of equations, as we sit in the sterile photographic laboratories with piously crossed telescopes) that the grand cosmic pattern at any rate will endure: galaxies, nebulae, orbits, ellipses, parallax and equinox, they are from everlasting to everlasting. A superbly chaste faith: but sufficently chastened? Our maps of the visible universe are projected on a heroic scale, but they do not commit the cosmic process to living up to the advance billing; and the algebraic hen-tracks across the map are not very mysterious, as to their origin or meaning.

We cannot successfully challenge the fact that the horizons of our knowledge of Nature have been pushed farther back. In our knowing Nature is truly an expanding universe. New structures of meaning rush in from the four corners. These accessions of knowledge, so far as they are that, but serve to deepen the riddles of existence and not to resolve them. We are able to make human life a great deal more comfortable than other generations dreamed was possible, or even desirable for that matter. Life expectancy in our society has been wonderfully extended; and sober men, inebriated with the sobriety of Science, wonder when, not whether, the human individual will be able to live forever; and countless people afflicted with mortally incurable diseases wait with bated breath for the news flash that the Cure has been found and they need not die. O, ye blessed generation to come, born of mortality but not to die, then weep for us whose fate it was to ask and try to reason *why?*, but no surcease to find save angrily to die.

In our world objective being has become a torrent of "new

meanings"—this we must say. *But nothing comes from objective being to illuminate the meaning of existence itself.* Without illumination of existence itself, life for us is infinitely burdensome; and when this is so, the prospect of endless existence is a horror in a class by itself.

Subjective Being and the Meaning of Existence

Then does the "answer" to the riddle of existence come from subjective being, which for us is fundamentally the principle of our person-hood? Surely, we have in ourselves the "meaning" of personal existence. Relative to the center of his activity, only the person "knows who he is", what he purposes, how he prefigures the world as the objective of his action, what possibilities he envisages, etc. Nevertheless, we do not find here, either, the meaning of *the fact of our existence.* Subjective being is a grasp upon the interior principle of activity, but we are not subjects who comprehend existence, just as we are not subjects who have power to bestow existence. That power is being itself. But again we encounter the "veil" of being itself. *Being itself is power and powers beyond all the structures of meaning within our grasp.*

Being present within this veil is the ground of abysmal terror. Abysmal terror is an appropriate response to immeasurable power of being which refuses to be held to reasonable account. When we see such power in human form we cannot afford to be paralyzed—we have to act (swiftly and ruthlessly) to protect society from the depradations of such monsters. But the instincts of civilization avail nothing against the pure power of being. "Repent" is sound counsel whenever it is true that "even now the axe is laid against the root of the tree". Persons and civilization have to undergo pruning operations from time to time—hard times overtake even the most rational economic orders, and for this and other (and perhaps better) reasons, individuals have to simplify and purify their lives. But what can be done, of saving grace, when the axe attacks the very roots of the tree of meaning? When fundamental values erode into nothing, and life becomes sterile routine and is stalked by other terrors that "wasteth at high noon"? In such a time many things are done, of course, but they are done more in despair than in hope. We say to ourselves, "keep your head, things will work out, think good thoughts, keep smiling, we've come through worse than this" etc., while the roof comes loose and sails away and the foundations collapse.

Being itself conceals itself within overpowering blasts of "non-being". Destructive forces assail what we had believed and hoped to be immovable and indestructible structures of meaning. These furious storms are of history, not of nature: they are manifest in human form, scourges, devastations, blights and abominations in the likeness of Man. Why do they so furiously rage? Perhaps if they had been nursed by breast rather than by synthetic nipple? Or had enjoyed a satisfactory sex-life? Or had not been afflicted with an authoritarian father? Or had been? Or had stayed in Sunday School? All these sandbags thrown against the floods are much too little applied belatedly at the wrong point. Why do they so furiously rage? Because "the people imagine a vain thing": that by taking thought, and after a moment or two of prayer to the familar domestic gods, dessicated forms of meaning can be restored to power and beauty. They will not face the bitter truth in which alone is the imperceptible seed of salvation. The truth is that humanly achieved structures of meaning have their own pulse of mortality—they have their day and cease to be, except in corrupted memories and imaginations, where they are impregnable and often sport a horrid power of infertile reproduction.

Being veiled within the *NO!* to creaturely presumptions of everlastingness is a bristling affront to religious, or quasi-religious, notions of Providence, which seek to exhibit, in a formula, how God works out His benign intent in all the terrors both of Nature and of History. God there shines forth like a superior Police Magistrate, majestically proportioning punishment to desert, and taking full account of youthful propensities for the sowing of Wild Oats, in those who, with gentle remonstrance, will yet become Pillars of Society. We cannot say realistically that these stale intellectual vices are behind us, but we have hope. Suffering is too great and too much with us for such comfort. The desolation of hope and of courage and of sacrifice of self beyond the call-of duty, is all too real and too common to succumb to such sleazy blandishment; though scorn does less than justice to the posturing in the name of Providence—the histrionic gestures, the declamations that "God reigns and the Constitution of the United States will endure" etc.,—for, were it not for some wholly mysterious ordering of persons and events, we should still be found rooted and grounded in such folly.

Personal Signifance and Being Itself

Our account of the "veils of being itself" ought also to include *solicitation by being itself but without manifest fulfilment by being itself*. "Abysmal terror" is not the only appropriate response of the creature to the "depths and heights" of pure being. There is also in us a sense of being "under summons" by powers greater than ourselves, and of being solicited for ends not of our own choosing. This awareness is exploited, exacerbated and painfully inflamed by popular teaching to the effect that the Heart of the Universe has a personal interest in every person, as in every blade of grass and every feather of every bird. Popular religion (here as everywhere in its broad and cluttered domain) is devised to comfort and console by administration of mild, though habit-forming anesthetic, a treatment deemed especially desirable and salutary where frustration with the Heart of the Universe appears likely to make for a poor adjustment to society. In the present age we see how the anesthetics are wearing off— slowly but surely. No doubt others are in the making, but they will have to be good to recover for religious institutions ground lost to the deepest and most unrelenting enemy of all, being itself. For the frustrations inflicted by being itself are wholly real and painful.

I do not mean to suggest seriously that all frustrations are to be laid at the feet of being itself. One's view of the world, and his readiness to come to some amicable terms with it, are not greatly improved by seeing in falling hair, swelling girth and collapsing arches, so many personal visitations of Almighty demonry. But over against all the natural vicissitudes and outrages to which we are subjected, and not as their total or sum, we do and must endure being summoned to resolutions and ventures where failure, ruin, and death await us. Being so imperiously summoned, we go forth not knowing whither we go; and if piety assures us that angels, breathing sweet beneficence, everywhere accompany us in that pilgrimage, we have a surer sense that The Furies are at least as attentive and are somewhat more successfully adjusted to the rigors of the march, than the messengers of Heaven. Of old it has been said, "we are not tempted beyond our power". The doctrine is false. We are tempted both by things immensely hurtful to life and to self-respect, and by things wonderfully enriching to life and spirit, if they could be attained without jeopardy to things which far more certainly lie within our powers. We do not have an infallible knowledge that temptations of the second order would be good for us and for the race, but lack of such knowledge concerning the things within our competence (and the lack is real) is not a reasonable ground for inactivity or irresolution. The more important point is not a meaningless desire to be sure of success in impossible ventures, but a desire for a disclosure of being itself. So far as we are reasonably proud we do not want to be gulled, even by our own "best instincts". We want more than patience to endure a world which threatens to precipitate itself into astonishing meaningfulness only to withdraw within the veil of mystery. We will not deny or cavil: if our existence itself is "summons", then our being is invested with the possibility of a certain terrestrial glory. But this works two ways: if "summons" is but a word to dignify our own inwardly-legislated constraints and our self-instruction, it is feckless posturing and there is no health in it.

Veiled being, in sum, is the near and omnipresent mystery, rather than the remote ranges of being lightly sketched by speculation: questions without "answer", terrors without proportioned comfort, "temptations" without power either to ignore or to attain.

BEING UNVEILED

Serious religious thinking is motivated by a desire to know truly rather than by a desire to get the tradition-truth of a religious community down the throat of an unbelieving generation against its better judgment. So far as it is "religious" thinking it is *committed*, which is to say both that it is powered and permeated with passion and that it is something going on in a circle of similarly devoted people, to whose best interests the thinking man would be loyal. But loyalty is best when it is discriminating—no one is properly honored or otherwise enhanced by being the recipient of "blind" loyalty. And what is true for personal relations is true also of respect for traditions of religious communities. Say, if you please, that truth is in a tradition; but the whole truth is not there, and the tradition is not the pure truth except by presumption. For serious religious thinking, the tradition is the occasion for enquiry and reflection: we must take thought to learn how to express what we know but also to *know* where we have only surmised, presumed and believed.

Tradition-truth and Being Itself

The root and ground of tradition-truth[1] in religion are being itself. This does not mean that the beliefs of a given religious

---

1. "Tradition-truth" is awkward and perhaps uninformative. I use it because "truths" are part of every religious community's life and because these "truths" are always received from the past in some degree or another.

community are a necessary and inevitable expression of being itself, as though being had but one word for all history and had uttered it in perfect syntactical and logical detail at some point in the past. We mean simply to note that being itself is the objective of tradition-truth, being is what such truths are about. Religious traditions are ostensibly concerned with being only so far as being is divine, or only so far as human existence and Deity have to put up with each other (on the basis of certain valuable considerations). Here appearances are misleading. Nothing is commoner in higher religion than a distinction between true gods and false gods; and the distinction is there proposed on the assumption of an unquestionably authentic disclosure of the truth of being. Thus religious tradition is revered, and treasured beyond all goods and truths of earth, because God is disclosed in it, and not simply because of man's inveterate habit of believing that his greatness is somewhere behind him in the past. "Revelation" is the generic and inclusive name for God's self-disclosure. Our present purpose is to indicate how revelation may be understood as the unveiling of being.

Observe, first, that "reality" is inadequate to the demands of religion and that *being* is what religion needs. Every religion that is more than a merely plausible effort to bilk the world of some measure of responsibility and care due it, is greatly involved with "unrealities", that is, with the non-actual, as every such religious venture comes also to terms with "the threats of non-being". "Reality" has, for us, the feel and aroma of ancient idealisms—of things affirmed as true because desired by "spiritual" forces as edifying. We do not enter the lists against edification, until it is offered as a substitute, or remedy, for love of truth. Surely religion is not a natural enemy of that passion. To the contrary, religion at its best is a preparation for life in the truth. "You shall know the truth" is a *religious* promise, after all! And what is the hope of salvation if it is not the hope of "renewing drafts of being" offered us by God most truly divine?

God so invoked is being beyond the subjective-objective distinction, as we have drawn this distinction. If there are "appearances" within which God moves, none of these appearances is itself divine; and if God is the subject signified by *all* meanings, His essence is none of them, and neither is it any kind of sum or total of all such meanings. Hence we say that though God is the perfection of the power of knowing and of knowability, He is not known to us as objective being; though to this we must add that objective being "intends" God as being itself.

As God is beyond the subjective-objective distinction, so also is He beyond other characterizations of being, such as "general" and "specific". In the usual sense of the word *entity*, God is not an entity; He is not something to be enumerated as belonging to a class of individuals. But on the other hand God is not a *trait* or *characteristic* of all beings and all being, since *traits etc.* are the qualities and effects of power and of power itself.

We are saying that God is not to be understood in certain ways, but the fact is that many religious people believe that God *is* one or more of the things here denied, and many other things as well which we should deny upon hearing them. Why are we privileged to deny what so much of piety, and that so perfervid, has affirmed? The question is asked to clarify our objective and method. The objective is to determine under what kind of philosophic general-ization a very considerable variety of claims concerning revelation might be ordered, since we can hardly estimate the truth of claims until we know what is proposed by them. The method is to interpret claims made about the revelation of God as in substance claims made about being itself exhibited and exemplified in special rela-tionships to human existence. Total justice to all the claims, and to all the personal nuances of meaning in religious feeling and belief, it were presumption to strive for in such an account.

God as Truth

Now the claim before us is that *God is truth,* so far as God is beyond subjective and objective and is the " convergence" of objective and subjective. Does this mean that the proposition, *God is truth,* is of the same order as the proposition, for example, *God is just?* Apparently, but only apparently.*God is just* is a "characterizing proposition" (*judgment* we should say), very much of the order of *John's nose is red,* except of course for the difference in nobility of the subject of the proposition. On the other hand, *God is truth* can hardly be a characterizing proposition, except in appearance, because "truth" is *not* a property or characteristic; and it is not the real intent of the proposition *God is truth* to treat truth as a property etc. *That real intent is to identify being itself as divine: truth is of the essence of God.* Thus the proposition *God is truth* is a proposi-tion of essential attribution.

But what does *God is truth* mean? Some will say, it means that God is an utterly reliable moral agent whose word is as good as his bond. This is to interpret truth as integrity or sense of honor. But there is meaning in attributing moral integrity to God only so far as there is clear and compelling reason for first attributing moral agency to him. Such a reason must be grounded in being itself rather than in something in the heart of man desiring comfort and companionship in high places. We do not deny that such reasons may be brought forward. We are saying that such reasons must employ the notion of truth, and of God as truth, in a sense significantly different from truth as moral integrity. *God is truth* is then a proposition about being itself and not, in the first instance, about a recognizably moral agent greater then ourselves.

So we ask again, what does *God is truth mean?* It means that the mystery of being itself is unveiled at a given point by the power of being itself. Now to say that the mystery of being is unveiled is not to say that the mystery is removed in such a way that being itself becomes part of the standard furnishings of the mind of the knower. (The *concept* of being itself is part of the furnishings of the mind, but this does not mean that the full being of being itself has its dwelling-place there.) Authentic mystery is not dispelled. Its "unveiling" is its assuming a particular form through which the powers of being rain (or shine, if that metaphor seems more appropriate rather than merely more familiar) directly upon creaturely spirit. This directness of presentation, this immediacy of "presence", activates the essential powers of creaturely spirit who is the recipient of the revelation. What he knows of God in this moment of acute awareness is "beyond knowing", which means that normal knowledge does not apprehend such a moment and that being disclosed through it is not an ordinary "object of knowledge". The mind is too full of meaning, is too largely blessed with meaning, to be concerned with "knowing", so far as that process involves relating meanings presented in awareness to established structures of meaning; and so far as it involves the act of judgment, that act of attribution of meanings to a subject. In the moment of revelation the presented meanings are overwhelming; and the Subject of attribution does not appear as such as in them, but is 'beyond' them, controlling them and 'judging' them.

What is the *moment of revelation?* What is the *unveiling?* Much of the evidence of religious experience converges to suggest that the *moment* is one of extraordinary clarification of the person's being. The "meaning of existence" becomes all but unbearably clear, not as the final working-out or confirmation of a world-view or philosophy of life but as a summons to be acted upon and acted out. One feels that he is summoned and that he will be sustained by power from beyond himself in his 'answer'. He knows that the *reason for his existence* is concealed somewhere in his own powers of being and will be made manifest only by his own resolution.

In the *moment of revelation* being assumes a "particular form". Being itself in this sense "appears". But what is this sense? Note first that in this moment the mind attends to *something* and not to nothing. Something is given to it. (The person does not "take leave of his senses"—his powers of percipience are greatly intensified.) What is given may be a form of ordinary experience—a flying cloud, a pewter kettle, the bodily form of a human being—prediction of the particular form is folly, save where religious communities prestructure events (really, *interpretation* of events). But we must also note, secondly, that in the *moment* the standard day-to-day interpretation of the form is overcome as the form is

freighted with the "meaning" of being itself. The form takes on an
intentional life and power of its own, but not so much its own as
of being itself. The mortal mind cannot trace the relationships
running from the form to the ultimate subject of all attribution;
and we sometimes accordingly declare that no such relationships are
there; but we also sometimes believe that God has chosen that form
for our illumination and salvation, in a way roughly similar to that
in which we choose the proper reading matter for our children. Yet
whatever our attitude about the relationship of form to the intent of
being itself, the relationship is not given as the particular form
itself is. After the moment of revelation many possibilities of interpretation appear, and a choice must be made, and is made, from
among them. But the same constraint and inducement to decision
about the adequate pattern of interpretation cannot be successfully
traced into the *moment* itself, because the summons and inducement of the *moment* draws upon the essential power of being in the
person rather than especially upon his power of thinking and his
power of believing. One decides to become a Christian in the sense
of identifying oneself with the christian community as a repository
of interpretative schematisms, in a way fundamentally different from
the way in which he grasps in "Christ" the meaning of his existence.

Truths and "Truths"

At this point a shrieking paradox strikes at us as a falcon
slashes at an innocent cotton-tail. We bare our heads to it: If *God
is truth* is true, the "content" of revelation cannot be "truths"
(true teachings about God, Man, Nature, etc). One reason for
this astounding conclusion is that "truths" about being are thought-

out interpretations of concrete events and are therefore not the immediate 'message' of such events. Now the *moment of revelation* is such an event; hence "truths" about God etc., are "after the fact", though they are (in intent) about the fact and are occasioned by the fact. One may assert that the power of God which grasped one in the *moment* is veritably the same as that power now constraining the mind to believe certain things about God so revealed. Nothing is known about God or about being which demands an automatic denial of this claim. On the other hand nothing is generally known which supports it in a clear and compelling manner. Moreover, the claim frequently rests upon a confusion of *revelation* with *inspiration*. Inspiration is the name for a feeling that one has been guided by a power beyond himself to believe and to express certain things. If the pun is not too offensive, an inspired person is a be-Mused person, which is to say, one upon whom the "spirit" of an occasion rests as an agent to a desired end. So we commonly say that a person is *inspired* when he brings off something he would not ordinarily have been thought capable of. Thus the *moment of revelation* may prompt someone, as he reflects upon it, to express himself as he judges he would not have been able to do by himself. He may become a prodigy of creativity—he may sing like an angel or love like a saint, etc.

We are not saying that "truths" about God are mere afterthoughts or incidental by-products of revelation, but only that such truths do not relate persons to being as revelation itself does. This difference does not follow simply from the fact that the believing community prompts the formulation of teachings about God and passes on their acceptability, though this is true in general. We are not quite prepared to say that the *moment of revelation* is an exclusively individual affair, though there is much "witness" to support that contention. The believing community is in the picture very early and stays in it very late. Indeed this community figures so prominently in Western religion that one can easily feel that the Community regulates the "veils of being" very much as though they were proscenium curtains given into its charge. Symbols assume there a normative quality. Words and gestures are standardized and stabilized; and people assume that these are the nets which capture the Holy Spirit, within a small and predictable margin of error. Sound doctrine and its acceptance as true attain the stature of conditions of membership in the Kingdom of God. In a word, the truths of religion absorb God as truth.

If we ask, What is the driving power within such developments in the name of God, we answer: Anxiety. And anxiety of a particular quality. *In the believing community people are anxious over the thrusts and flights of being beyond their gods.* Another way of saying this is: the community knows that if revelation is true, the truths of the community are only derivately, not absolutely, true; and that the process of derivation is subject to multitudinous error. For revelation as the *moment* is certainly not true in the sense in which propositions descriptive of fact or propositions expressing purely formal relationships, can be judged true or false. Moments, whether sublime or trival, occur. Things happen in them, and meanings are presented to minds through these events. The *moment of revelation,* we have argued is an occasion in which the mystery of being assumes a form so palpably imperative that the mortal participant in the *moment* feels his very being under "summons". Unveiling discloses the meaning of his existence. But God does not disclose His own essence in that *moment*. If the *moment* matters greatly to God it does not make the same difference to Him that it makes to the person caught up in it. And so the truths which try to comprehend both God as such and the meaning of revelation are all derivative and are all complex and compound derivatives. An ethical code is one such derivative. Creedal formulae are another derivative. Institutional organization is another. And each of these is in itself a compound and complex derivative. The ethical codes of religious communities, to take that for an example, are compounds of imperatives derived from revelation and of elements drawn from the "best of pagan virtues" and of utilitarian adjustments. Moreover, the actual process of derivation of stabilized meanings from revelation is itself compounded of "inspiration", logic, and hard-headed common-sense. God is not known to look with active disfavor upon any of these components of religious "truths", but there is overwhelming evidence that He reveals no sense of obligation to sustain in perpetuity the works of our hands and minds.

Being "Re-veils" Itself

"Overwhelming evidence", yes, this is no exaggeration. The truth about being itself is that being itself "re-veils" before our eyes. The palpable form assumed by being itself in the *moment of revelation* is absorbed into standard patterns of knowledge. Crumbs fallen from the sacramental table are eaten by the dogs and the ants and they go their respective ways unedified. The *moment* is remembered and is elaborated and embellished by memory; and old-wives-tales become gospel-truth; and in the congregation diverse and sundry goodfellows and gooddames are inspired to arise and utter wondrous things; and solemn councils are summoned to see which of these utterances is canonical truth. In many such ways the mystery is institutionalized, which certainly makes it easier to live with.

But the re-veiling of being itself is very much more than our all-too human propensity for trivializing what we value most. Let us see the recedence of mystery rather in the fact that men cry out (in all humility and in unmistakable terror) for a "sign", for a sure witness in time of great trouble that "God is with us", and no sign is given. Power (truth and beauty) vanishes from venerable symbol, and our spirits wander in waterless places. Even if we could or had need to believe that we sin more heinously than our bible-quoting fathers, we cannot believe that unto us the power is given to exhaust the reservoirs of celestial mercy. Yet we hunger without hope for the truth of being.

Surely our thinking about God as the prime symbol of the religious community must come to grips with being itself. Nothing reasonable compels a loose or quick unity of "God" with being itself; but we must say that a God armed with less than the ultimate powers of being is a shaking reed. We have no certain clue as to how these are unified in being wholly divine—for this is not revealed. Revelation calls into action our essential powers; and their unity, in any important degree or quality, is an attainment of our freedom. We conclude from this (and actually from other things not brought under scrutiny in these discussions) that being self-disclosed in revelation is not only the ground both of our power and our freedom but is in Himself the perfection of freedom.

The Julian Hartt Library
Series Editor: Jonathan R. Wilson

*V.   A Christian Critique of American Culture: An Essay
        in Practical Theology* (1968).
        Introduction by David Kelsey.

Hartt's major work defies labels. The subtitle identities it as
"practical theology"; by that, Hartt means those doctrines
that have immediately to do with the church's mission to
proclaim the gospel. Those doctrines are presented in un-
precedented ways as Hartt engages in cultural analysis, an-
ticipates much that is found in "missional church" thinking,
exposits a Christology and anthropology simultaneously,
and sketches a theology of culture that equals any sociology
of culture.

VI.   The Restless Quest (1975).
        Introduction by Jonathan R. Wilson.

A collection of essays and addresses that argue for Hartt's
understanding of the task of theology of culture (Part I) and
the practice of theology of culture as the illumination of our
situation (Part II) and our politics (Part III) in the light of
Jesus Christ.

VII.   Theological Method and Imagination (1977).
        Introduction by Ray L. Hart.

Hartt applies his wit, insight, and critical acumen to questions ranging across metaphysics, truth, authority, history,
imagination and more.

*VIII. What We Make of the World: Memoirs of Julian
        Hartt (1998-99).*

In these memoirs, Julian Hartt practices the "cosmological
theology" that he calls for throughout his scholarly work
by reflecting on the everyday, ideal, and natural worlds of

his own life. These worlds are shaped by significant times, places, and persons. But most important is the unrelenting honesty of Hartt's narrative as it witnesses to the grace that makes truth and truthfulness possible and bearable in our broken world.

Contributors to The Julian Hartt Library

Ray L. Hart is Dean of the School of Theology and Professor of Religion and Theology at Boston University.

Stanley Hauerwas is Gilbert T. Rowe Professor of Theological Ethics at Duke Divinity School.

David H. Kelsey is Luther Weigle Professor of Theology Emeritus at Yale Divinity School.

Walter J. Lowe is Professor of Systematic Theology at Candler School of Theology, Emory University.

John D. Sykes, Jr., is Professor of English at Wingate University.

Jonathan R. Wilson is Professor of Theology and Ethics at Acadia Divinity College.